D1614282

Boise State College Western Writers Series   Number 4

Wallace Stegner

By Merrill and Lorene Lewis
Western Washington State College

Editors: Wayne Chatterton
James H. Maguire

Business Manager:
James Hadden

Cover Design and Illustration
by Arny Skov, Copyright 1972

Boise State College, Boise, Idaho

Printed in the United States of America by
The Caxton Printers, Ltd.
Caldwell, Idaho

Wallace Stegner

Wallace Stegner

WALLACE STEGNER has on several occasions described the situation of the Western, regional writer in terms that come remarkably close to describing his own work and his own career. In his essay "Born a Square" (*Atlantic,* Jan. 1964) he writes that the Western writer (as distinguished from the writer of "Westerns") is trapped by his "squareness" in his own peculiar box. Getting out—finding an audience and a way of writing—has its difficulties. His box is booby-trapped at one end because the region of his origins does not give him an adequate intellectual and artistic tradition within which to work. It is booby-trapped at the other end because the twentieth-century artistic and intellectual traditions that lie outside the region—and might offer a substitute—are inconsistent with his experience and potentially destructive of his art. To escape this dilemma, Stegner urges the young writer to go away from the West and get his eyes opened to the West's cultural and intellectual limitations and then look back to his region without becoming lost in its history or myths, or carried away by its scenic landscapes.

The advice carries the authority of one who has been there before. Stegner's own career has involved striking out on such an intellectual and literary adventure, and his return to the region of his origins is fraught with the dangers of provincialism, nostalgia, and historicism. Both the advice and the statement of the problem are typically Stegnerian. The central theme of all his work is the quest for identity, personal and regional, artistic and cultural.

He is a willing advocate, he says in "Fiction: A Lens on Life," of the so-called "personal heresy" (*Sat. Rev.*, April 22, 1950). What the reader seeks in fiction is probably himself and, being denied that, "the completely intimate contact which may show us another like ourselves." What we as readers discover, if the work of fiction has genuinely moved us, is the "refined and distilled spirit" of the writer, and "the totality of his understanding" (p. 32). But in the case of the regional writer these identifications are possible only if the writer confronts the past and the history that makes his own regional experience what it is. After "we have finished our most personal books," Stegner writes of himself and his generation of regional writers, "we have all taken refuge in history, fictionalized or straight" ("Born a Square," p. 48). The past can be, and often has been for Western writers, a sanctuary. The danger of such a return to the past, however, is that it may become self-congratulatory instead of self-revealing. The past must be understood as inseparable from the present before it may legitimately become the business of the writer of fiction:

> In the old days we used to tie a string of lariats from house to barn so as to make it from shelter to responsibility and back again. With personal, family, and cultural chores to do, I think we had better rig up such a line between past and present. ("History, Myth and the Western Writer," *Sound of Mountain Water*, p. 201)

The importance given here to personal experience makes Stegner's biography of particular interest to the student of his work. He was born in Lake Mills, Iowa, in 1909, the son of George H. and Hilda (Paulson) Stegner, Scandinavian immigrants. During the first twelve years of Stegner's life, his father attempted to maintain the family in such widely separate areas of the West as North Dakota, Washington, Saskatchewan, Montana, and Wyoming before settling the family in Salt Lake City in 1921. For the next nine years they lived in various places in that city—they moved some twelve times, Stegner later recalled. There young Stegner attended public school and the University of Utah, where he received a B.A. in 1930.

From Utah he went to the University of Iowa in Iowa City as a graduate student and part-time teacher. He received an M.A. from Iowa in 1932 and the Ph.D. in 1935. In the meantime he studied at the University of California at Berkeley in 1932 and 1933. Following his mother's death in 1934, he took a job for a brief time at Augustana College in Rock Island, Illinois, and married Mary Stuart Page. He returned to Utah as an instructor in the English Department in 1934, prior to completing the doctoral degree at Iowa.

Stegner remained on the staff at Utah only three years before moving on to the University of Wisconsin in 1937. Between 1939 and 1945 he was Briggs-Copeland Instructor of Composition at Harvard University. In 1945 he again returned West to take a position as Professor of English at Stanford University. The next year he became Director of the Creative Writing Program. Aside from years he spent on leave in Europe or the Orient on fellowships or while writing, and summers spent of late in Vermont—a state he discovered during his six years at Harvard—Stegner remained at Stanford until his retirement in 1971.

All his major writing is strongly regional, whether Western or not, reflecting his experiences in different sections of the country. His first novel, *Remembering Laughter* (1937), is set in Iowa farm country. Saskatchewan is the setting for *On a Darkling Plain* (1939), his third novel, and for *Wolf Willow* (1962), a reminiscence and a history of the southern Saskatchewan prairies. It is also the setting for a major portion of *The Big Rock Candy Mountain* (1943), the fifth and most clearly autobiographical novel, which actually covers much the same territory as that traveled by the Stegner family on their way to settling in Salt Lake City.

Stegner claims that the half-dozen years spent in Cambridge, Massachusetts, have left the least distinctive memories. But New England gave him material for his sixth novel, *Second Growth* (1947). A grant he received in 1953 from the Wenner-Gren Foundation for Anthropological Research for the study of village democracy in Saskatchewan, New England, and Denmark—a grant that allowed him to collect the material for *Wolf Willow*—indicates that the early novels, *Wolf Willow,* and the Mormon books, *Mormon Country* (1942) and *The Gathering of Zion* (1964), share much common ground—namely, Stegner's interest in regional folkways, the making of cultures and communities. These interests are also evident in his last three novels with their settings in contemporary California.

Obviously Stegner's long tenure at Stanford and his connection with academia generally are most difficult biographical matters to assess. His success as a teacher of creative writing, as well as his success as a writer, has given him opportunities and honors that not many regional writers have obtained. He has had access to major libraries for research; he has had the opportunity to travel and the leisure to write. In addition to the grant from the Wenner-Gren Foundation which enabled him to write *Wolf Willow,* he has twice, in 1950 and again in 1959, received Guggenheim fellowships. For the year 1950-1951 he received a Rockefeller fellowship to teach a seminar for writers in the Far East. His lectures delivered at Keio University in Tokyo, Japan, and collected in *The Writer in America* (1952) analyze American fiction in both its historical and contemporary contexts. In 1955-1956 he was a Fellow at the Center for Advanced Studies in Behavioral Sciences, and five years later, in 1960, he was Writer in Residence at the American Academy in Rome.

The imaginative center of Stegner's world includes the six years spent in Whitemud and on the southern plains of Saskatchewan, the sixteen years associated directly with Salt Lake City and Mormon Country, and the world of books and art. The region he imaginatively identifies with is roughly the intermountain West, the region designated by Brigham Young to be the Mormon Empire—with California, Washington, Saskatchewan, and the Midwest on the periphery. It is somewhat more extensively the semi-arid West that lies between the ninety-eighth meridian and the Pacific slope. Culturally it is dominated at the center by the Mormons. The "Gentiles" (Stegner is one) represent a transient, anarchic, and rootless contrast to the Mormon community.

Stegner tells us in *Wolf Willow* that he is conscious of a discrepancy in his own biography between "that part of me that reflects the folk culture and that part which reflects an education imported and often irrelevant" (p. 22). For the young boy Bruce Mason in *The Big Rock Candy Mountain* summer, the prairie, and the family homestead meant freedom, while winter and Whitemud meant school and the excitement of books.

For Stegner this dichotomy is merely an extension of the split between Europe and America, civilization and barbarism. The West of his youth provided evidence of the "rawest forms of deculturation," on the one hand, and "the most slavish respect for borrowed elegances," on the other (p. 23). Even the writer's style is shaped by both the prairie and school:

> Contradictory voices tell you who you are. You grow up speaking one dialect and reading and writing another. During twenty-odd years of education and another thirty of literary practice you may learn to be nimble in the King's English; yet in moments of relaxation, crisis, or surprise you fall back into the corrupted lingo that is your native tongue. Nevertheless all the forces of culture and snobbery are against your *writing* by ear and making contact with your own natural audience. Your natural audience, for one thing, doesn't read—it *isn't* an

audience. You grow out of touch with your dialect because learning and literature lead you another way unless you consciously resist. (*Wolf Willow*, p. 26)

In Stegner's stories, School and University are sometimes a sanctuary for boys trying to escape oppressive family environments, as in "The Blue-Winged Teal" and "The Volunteer," collected in *City of the Living* (1956), and in *Remembering Laughter* (1937) and *Second Growth* (1947). The classic case is that of Bruce Mason.

This is but another way of describing the "box" which the Western writer is trapped in. Whether or not it is an accurate description of the dilemma facing regional writers is not our task to determine. However, it describes the polarities that inform Stegner's work.

II

Stegner's early novels are short, possibly better called novellas. One was written as a result of one publishing house's attempt to popularize the short novel by conducting a contest. *Remembering Laughter* won the Little, Brown competition in 1937. *The Potter's House* (1938), *On a Darkling Plain* (1940), and *Fire and Ice* (1941) are equally limited in scope and equally concise. When contrasted with the breadth and depth of realism found in the later fiction and histories, these novels seem now to be un-Stegnerlike. Yet Stegner has written that the novella is a form especially good for telling the initiation story, the trial by ordeal or crisis involved in a boy's becoming a man. His later story "Genesis," included in *Wolf Willow*, is a good example of the form. These early novels involve a young person who is breaking away from the past, testing himself and certain "ideas" against realities of the human condition. They all reflect Stegner's humanistic bias.

In *Remembering Laughter* the community and Calvinistic puritanism combine to suppress the main characters, who cannot escape the consequences of their human inclinations and weaknesses. As in Edith Wharton's *Ethan Frome,* a vigorous man falls in love with his wife's sister, and all three are eventually doomed to live a cloistered life, with a double burden of guilt for the erring couple and stiff self-righteousness for the wronged wife. The book opens with the husband's funeral, a scene of brittle austerity, and then gives us a long flashback to warmer sunlit days of too-brief laughter on the Iowa farm where prosperous farmer Alec MacLeod and his wife Margaret have been joined by her immigrant sister Elspeth from Scotland. Elspeth seems to share a kind of pagan yeomanism with Alec. Her debut in the prim household, the robust farm scenes, the early gaiety of the young people, Alec's imaginative tall tales, stiff but charming party scenes, and bursts of intimate passion that finally overcome restraint are the memorable scenes in the book. When Margaret stumbles onto their betrayal and then learns that her sister is pregnant, she pragmatically sends away a hired workman so that the sin is compounded by dishonesty. Margaret will not brook complete disgrace, the only real alternative. The child of the union, Malcolm, will grow up in this house without knowing who his parents are, deprived of the warmth he might have known, and will leave the farm as a young man to escape the essential dishonesty of it all.

People set apart from society by physical difference as well as conduct are the subject of *The Potter's House,* a novella published in a limited edition of 490 copies in 1938. The potter is a sensitive deaf mute whose talents barely earn subsistence for his wife and children as he works through long sunny California afternoons. Although his wife, Annie, is also handicapped and not very bright, she is a satisfied and devoted wife, mother of

11

their four children, and vendor of her husband's wares. Their life is nearly content, the only dissonant note coming from Annie's resentment toward the one child who can hear. The potter insists upon music lessons for Mabel's prodigious talent, an unheard-of extravagance in the frugal household.

Then, goaded by the insecurity he feels when his deaf children are stared at or taunted by others, the potter agrees to his brother's suggestion that he submit to voluntary sterilization. Annie, feeling the implied slight, rejects him completely and leaves the home. Within two weeks she is jailed for drunken and indecent behavior. She stolidly scorns the potter's offer of reconciliation, and leaves him the task of managing alone, of facing the breakup of his household. What seemed a simple solution to his brother, and a necessary one to the potter, turned out to be no solution at all, and opened a Pandora's box without hope at the bottom.

On a Darkling Plain, published in the terrible war years of 1939-1940, presents in simple outline the theme binding the individual to the human community. Because the plot turns so dramatically upon the great flu epidemic of 1918, the novel shows a strong resemblance to Albert Camus' later, more complex novel, *The Plague,* which also asserts that we are all victims of our common mortality, and that the best of mankind will always seek to stay on the side of the victim in this universally shared catastrophe, remaining neither aloof nor uninvolved.

Edwin Vickers, a young soldier recovering from a gas attack on a nearly decimated Canadian regiment during World War I, seeks solitude by homesteading on a Saskatchewan plain, in order to heal lungs and spirit, both equally damaged by the horror of war. He seeks escape from the war memories, "the lotus-land" of his home and solicitous mother, and the nosiness of the Canadian villagers who sense that he is "different." His bent for Thoreauvian solitude is immediately undone when Vickers finds himself unable to subsist on his homestead without help from neighbors; and drawn to their adolescent daughter, touched by her loneliness, he shares his books with her, reading to her Matthew Arnold's "Dover Beach," about receding faith in God and man, "ignorant armies that clash by night," and human fidelity.

The tension of the story develops between Vickers' desire for solitude and his need for companionship and communication, his retreat to the prairies and his restlessness when there, the paralysis of will and the need for physical productivity. He finds himself trapped by conflicting desires and cursed with a conscience. He senses that evil is down "in his burrow" with him. Though the scenes of nature on the Canadian prairies are drawn with almost mystical intensity, Vickers is made to discover in mid-novel that he cannot write poetry only about the vastness of nature surrounding him—but that he needs the human figure on the landscape to complete its meaning.

When the plague of influenza sweeps over the prairie provinces, the human community joins forces against it, and the homesteaders go in to town to fight it out together. Vickers goes, without question, to the aid of his neighbors. Inspired by human laughter in the face of absurdity, he denies even his own grief and sickness to help the good young doctor and to bury the dead.

Fire and Ice, unlike the other novels, lacks intimate contact with the land and stands somewhat apart—just as the college community in which it is set exists in a kind of isolation. The story chronicles the rise and fall of a student radical, Paul Condon, who in the early days of World War II German expansionism confines his concerns to working his way through school by holding four jobs and by supporting the Young Communist League with ten percent of his scant earnings and all the time left over from his unenviably tight schedule. His motivation for such devotion seems to be the memory of his sacrificial mother whose ill-paid work as scrubwoman drives him to seek more equitable economic answers to injustice.

His monkish determination is undone when he finds himself both attracted to and repelled by a young and lovely and well-to-do student. When she asks to interview him for a story on working students for the school paper he is inspired to clean his shabby room and to buy a bottle of whiskey, even though in two-and-a-half years of school his greatest extravagance has been a cup of coffee; he has never had a date. The interview ends in a violently surprising scene (foreshadowing those in later novels), as Paul's incredibly tight discipline is undone by the combination of alcohol and pent-up jealous resentment. Next, quickly to jail and quickly out of town with the help of his more uncomely but loyal and loving communist girl friend. Paul is resigned to leaving collective communist efforts and devoting himself to solitary soul-searching and to the examination of other than purely economic aspects of life.

This rejection of closed systems is characteristic of the short novels and illustrates Stegner's early conservatism regarding any ready-made radical political or utopian economic solutions to human inequities, a theme he picks up later in his novel on the life of Joe Hill, *The Preacher and the Slave* (1950), and in the latter part of *Angle of Repose* (1971). The portrayal of the self-destructiveness of Calvinism in *Remembering Laughter,* the failure of isolationist Thoreauvian individualism in *On a Darkling Plain* both indicate, too, that Stegner expects the human lot to be a complex one, without formulas for success. Characteristically, each of these novels ends with a young protagonist still outward bound in search of the self, hopeful of discovering new frontiers.

III

Stegner's fifth novel, *The Big Rock Candy Mountain* (1943), achieved immediate success. It develops many of the themes of the early novels, but the scope of events is much broader and the texture of reality much denser than in the earlier novels. Howard

14

Mumford Jones called it "a vast living untidy book." And yet the world which gives birth to the major characters, Harry and Elsa Mason and their boys Chet and Bruce, is completely realized and believable (*Sat. Rev.,* Oct. 2, 1943, p. 11).

Rather than relate the story of the Mason family by one long flashback, as he had done in *Remembering Laughter,* Stegner makes *The Big Rock Candy Mountain* a chronicle, beginning with the brief but passionate courtship of Elsa and Bo in Hardanger, North Dakota, at the turn of the century and ending with their deaths (from disease and suicide) some thirty years later. The novel repeats the earlier theme of youthful rebellion. Elsa flees to her uncle's house in Hardanger after her father has decided to marry her best friend following the difficult death of his wife. Bo Mason, who keeps a tavern in the town, has earlier escaped a child-beating father. Elsa accepts Bo's marriage proposal, despite her discovery that he can be brutal, because her father, concerned for propriety, tells her Bo does not seem respectable. Before the end of the novel their sons will repeat the pattern. The older son, Chet, elopes with a young girl who wants desperately to escape a repressive home life; and the younger son, Bruce, escapes to law school.

Between these cycles the family lives on the road, in pursuit of the father's dream of the Big Rock Candy Mountain. The dream is first articulated by Pinky Jordan, a drunk who buys his drinks at Bo's blind pig in Grand Forks, North Dakota, with gold dust he made in a killing in the Klondike Gold Rush. He is full of stories of "God's Country. Flowin 'th milk and honey." And he leaves behind "a vision of clean wilderness, white rivers and noble mountains, forests full of game and fabulously valuable fur, and sand full of glittering grains" (p. 92). He reminds Bo that all the good places are not used up, that there is still country where one can find the good life if one has the gumption and is willing to take chances.

The dream that Bo Mason pursues for the remainder of the

novel is more than the dream of the bitch goddess Success. It is the "dream of taking from life exactly what you wanted," and the quest for the Promised Land. The family fails to get to Alaska because illness holds them up in Seattle until news comes that the Klondike bubble has burst. Bo buys a small cafe in Richmond, Washington, in the middle of the rich timber country, and the family lives in a tent and dreams of a real house. A violent quarrel over Bo's mistreatment of Bruce leads to separation, and Bo next tries running a bunkhouse on wheels during the construction of a Canadian Pacific Railroad spur line in Saskatchewan, Canada. He finds brief success in this "new country," builds Elsa her dream house at the end of the line—Whitemud—and tries his luck in the new wheat bonanza by homesteading on the Saskatchewan prairies.

Elsa, forced to ignominious retreat to her father's home in Minnesota, is reconciled to a second chance in the spring of 1914. But by the fall of 1918, after a series of disastrous droughts, Bo admits that the homestead and the town are both "played out." Then, with the town on the verge of being invaded by the flu epidemic, Bo heroically travels across the line to the States in a blizzard—to get medicinal whiskey—and finds himself back in the liquor business. For the remainder of his life he is pursued alternately by the law and his dreams. And the pace of the novel is the movement between moments of family peace and reconciliation followed by quarrels and family upheaval. Elsa remains loyal to Bo, but unreconciled to their life. As mother and wife she is willing to sacrifice everything without losing her integrity. She yearns for friends and neighbors and goes without them.

Much of the early novel is told from the point of view of either Elsa or Bo. As the boys grow up, they add their points of view to the chronicle. Gradually, as first Chet and then Elsa die, Bruce carries more and more of the narrative. There are long reflective sections where he puzzles over the events of their

16

lives and, particularly, the paradoxical figure of his father. From his mother he has learned that there are things ten times worse than being poor. For the most part his reflections on his father's character are vindictive and motivated by hatred. What he wants is a moral justification for what he, Chet, and his mother have had to accept from his father. His desire for retribution may explain why he has selected law for a profession.

But there are several traits in his father that he cannot help admiring. In his father's fabulous imaginative capacity there is something of the raw, unformed poet. Bruce has that same imaginative capacity. On his way back West after his first year in law school (and before he has had to watch the slow, agonizing death of his mother and the cowardice of his father) , he sees himself first as "just a boll weevil lookin' for a home" and then as a Westerner who identifies with the same dream as his father. "He had a notion where home would turn out to be, for himself as for his father—over the next range, on the Big Rock Candy Mountain, that place of impossible loveliness that pulled the whole nation westward." He would accept the same gamble that his father accepted. "There were so many chances, such lovely possibilities" (pp. 423-25) .

And he is pleased to discover in himself some of his father's toughness as well as some of his mother's sensitivity. But to explain his father's failure seems an impossible task. Partly it was in Bo's nature. Partly, too, it came—as did his dream and his unbounding energy—from his pioneer forebears. "I suppose," Bruce writes in his journal, "that the understanding of any person is an exercise in genealogy." His father's ancestors, as far back as he could recollect, were pioneers, but his father was born "when almost all the opportunities for pioneering were gone" (pp. 403-04) . Bo Mason's tragedy, then, lies in the fact that his virtues were his undoing. Pioneer virtues have become twentieth-century man's vices.

At one point in *The Big Rock Candy Mountain* Bruce ponders

17

his family's isolation: "You've never paid an income tax [he tells his father]. . . . Two of us have never voted and the other one voted once, thirty years ago. Since I was born we've lived in two nations, ten states, fifty different houses. Sooner or later we're going to have to take out naturalization papers" (p. 443). There is a strong sense in this novel of what it is like to live beyond the pale.

The novel was published during World War II when more than one group in the United States was forced to test the strength of its "naturalization papers." The editors of *Look* magazine, aware in 1943 of what seemed to be a growing wave of intolerance in the country, asked Stegner to write a text to accompany a vivid photographic study of prejudice at work among several groups: the Filipinos, Japanese, Chinese, Mexican Americans, American Indians, Negroes, Catholics, and Jews. The book that emerged was *One Nation* (1945).

Stegner's text develops Gunnar Myrdal's theory that fear underlies prejudices. An initial fear leads one group or race to press upon another, deny it opportunities, and segregate it. When segregation lasts over any length of time and extends through many areas of experience (education, jobs, housing) it tends to create in the "inferior" race poverty, disease, and, perhaps, a compensatory "pushiness" which reinforces the original prejudice. While Stegner's prose sometimes suggests a certain "we-they" attitude towards these groups, his central thesis is that the nation is faced with a national problem and that the international hope for peace may turn out to be another "yeasty dream" unless peace and harmony can be achieved within one nation first.

It is not hard to guess why Stegner's next novel emerged after *One Nation*. In *Second Growth* (1947), a novel set in a New England village, Stegner narrows his "lens of vision" in order to examine in microcosm the problem of assimilation. In the prefatory note Stegner implies the universality of his setting, denying the painstaking care with which he has marked out the New

England landscape. He insists that the village could exist near Carmel or Taos, as well as in New Hampshire or Maine. "These people and their village took form in my mind not as portraits," personal or geographical, "but as symbols."

The symbols in the novel include the village itself, an antagonist of historic and traditional rigidity which poses problems for three characters who fight its stultifying influences by leaving it through death and departure or by joining it in assimilation and change, as an astute reviewer, Richard Sullivan (*The New York Times*, July 27, 1947), points out.

The character who chooses death as an escape from the village which ties her too closely to conformity is Helen, whose one experience in freedom (besides college) involves an aggressive lesbian friend. Helen cannot face life as village schoolteacher or as companion to aging parents who are symbolically paralytic and puritanical. Nor can she accept the utter abandonment of all restraint suggested by her new friend.

Another protagonist, Abe Kaplan, is an immigrant Jewish tailor whose patrons are for the most part the "summer people" —professor-folk who respect him for his intellectual interests and his religious and social independence. When he convinces a visiting Brooklyn Jewess to marry him, he forsakes the tent in which he has camped on the periphery of the village, builds a house, and seeks to become a part of the town. Ruth, his wife, sickens physically over the social isolation that ensues, until his heroic attempt to save Helen from suicide wins him some recognition and the couple a small degree of social acceptance.

These characters are tied to the third protagonist, the young boy Andy, through mutual acquaintance with a history professor, who offers Andy a chance to go away to school. Andy's alternative is apprenticeship to a fine old village artisan. The choice is made for him when the old man suffers a paralytic stroke. Andy leaves for school while looking back on the village with "the spectral taste of blackberries on his lips and his eyes already homesick for the autumn woods and the mown meadows . . . for the limited responsibilities and the wornout obligations and the narrow security that it would be fatal to accept" (p. 240). The history professor enunciates the theme—he visits the paralyzed craftsman who suffered the stroke, and is reminded that time is not forever, that the flexibility and freedom of one's own body is only a temporary accident of history. A sense of mortality and human illness brings all the characters to grips with the need for change, for adaptation, for a second growth when stasis has begun in any society.

IV

Implicit in Bruce Mason's reflections upon his father's character and the reasons for his father's failure in *The Big Rock Candy Mountain* is an invitation to someday write a history of his father's father, or, perhaps, a history of pioneer America. But Bruce is primarily concerned about justifying his father, not writing a family chronicle. Wallace Stegner has not written a systematic history of the pioneer or the frontier experience, either. However, he has written several books (both history and fiction) that make a contribution towards such a history.

Stegner's first book on the Mormons (*Mormon Country,* 1942) was written for the American Folkways Series edited by Erskine Caldwell, and the second (*The Gathering of Zion,* 1964) is Stegner's contribution to The American Trails Series edited by A. B. Guthrie. A novel about the Wobbly martyr Joe Hill, *The Preacher and the Slave* (1950), and a biography of John Wesley Powell, *Beyond the Hundreth Meridian* (1954), examine the lives of two distinctive Western characters who were dreamers and rebels. *Wolf Willow* (1962) is a history and a personal memoir of life on the southern Saskatchewan prairies, supplemented by several stories utilizing that locale.

One reviewer, Maureen Whipple, called *Mormon Country* "a potpourri of tales, legends, and impressionistic sketches—a sort of literary salad" (*Sat. Rev.,* Jan. 2, 1943, p. 21). In its heterogeneous mixture this work shares something structurally with *Wolf Willow.* The literary element of the book is demonstrated in the opening section, "Meet Me at the Ward House," a fictional account of how a cowboy named Milton takes his girl to a farewell dance given at a Mormon Ward House for a missionary soon to depart for Brazil. Stegner's object is to give the reader a sense of the importance of the Ward House as the center of Mormon social life. He prefers the concreteness of fiction to the more abstract exposition of historical prose. It puts the reader into immediate touch with the Mormon sense of community. He uses much the same technique later in the book when he gives a brief portrait of a Mormon family reunion, dramatizing the importance of the family in Mormon culture. The Mormon family finds its force in Mormon theology, which necessitates the study of genealogy and the keeping track of one's own.

Stegner is interested in the "peculiar" institutions of Mormon culture as well as the representative ones, polygamy and utopian experiments such as the one at Orderville (promoted by the United Order of Enoch). In the case of polygamy, he points out that there were still "fossil remains" of this supposedly defunct institution as late as 1942.

Because institutions have art forms, Stegner looks for those peculiar to Mormon country. Mormon culture produced a body of stories that fall somewhere between myth and legend, and these stories reflect the strange relationship of natural and supernatural phenomena found in stories in the *Book of Mormon.* The reputation of Jacob Hamblin, the Mormon Leatherstocking, and the legends of the Welsh Indians and the Nephite Patriarchs suggest the range of folklore native to Mormon culture.

Gentile life in Mormon country (the subject of the short, second part of the book) stands in stark contrast to the order, dis-

cipline, and sobriety characteristic of Mormon life. The fate
of the Gentiles was perhaps foreshadowed in the fate of Corinne,
the "Berg on the Bear," the Gentile city built at the northern end
of the Salt Lake Valley (to replace Mormon power with Gentile
power). Despite an energetic citizenry and momentary success,
the town gradually melted away and then, ironically, was transformed into "a sleepy Mormon village." Non-Mormons were
more successful in gaining economic control of the mining in-
dustry, but their major community enterprise, the jerry-built
town of Bingham, reflects the anarchic and exploiting interests
of the cultural minority. Such legendary characters as Rafael
Lopez, the outlaw who could not be captured, and Butch Cassidy
and the Wild Bunch offer a colorful contrast to the "dynamic,
dedicated, regimented, group-conscious and Heaven-conscious
people" (p. 281) who dominated the region.

The subject of Stegner's second book on the Mormons, *The
Gathering of Zion,* is the contrast between the "stylized memory of
the [Mormon] trail" as it exists in Mormon consciousness and the
experience of the trail as a human and historical event. For the
Mormons the Millennium and Manifest Destiny turned out to
be two versions of the same thing. The Mormon Pioneer and the
Mormon Trail carry as much force as the beehive in symbolizing
the fruits of labor and communal cohesiveness. The journey of a
people across the plains from Nauvoo to Salt Lake Valley was "a
rite of passage" to Zion and the Promised Land (pp. 1, 5). The
dream that sustained the Latter Day Saints on their journey was
the sacred variant of Bo Mason's secular dream. The Mormon
quest was also undertaken in the faith that the good country was
not all used up; that there was somewhere over the divide a sanctuary from the painful experiences, even failures, of the past.
For the Mormons the sanctuary meant escape from Gentile per-
secution in Missouri and Illinois.

Stegner's admiration for the heroism of the pioneer effort is
apparent throughout the narrative. The success of the migra-

tion of these people demonstrated the force of their faith and the rewards of the social organization and the discipline imposed by their leader Brigham Young. These people were not frontier scum, insisted the sympathetic but objective observer Thomas Kane, upon whose authority Stegner depends. They were not drifters, "but people in movement, a community and even a culture on the march—by all odds the most civilized element on that raw frontier" (p. 81).

But the experience of the trail perfected that organization and discipline, and measured the pioneers' human weaknesses. In such a human enterprise as the gathering of Zion there were bound to be victims and scapegoats as well as heroes. Stegner presents the human side of the Mormon Exodus most effectively by the use of two particular techniques. He lets the pioneers speak for themselves through their journals, diaries, letters, and reminiscences, and thus allows them to expose their anger, their frustrations, and even their pettiness, as well as their faith. And he focuses on certain events that offered the severest tests to both the church leadership and their faithful followers. The first of these is the rescue of the last of the Nauvoo refugees from Poor Camp and their removal at the end of a two-year struggle to build a road west across Iowa to Winter Quarters on the Missouri in order to move the Saints beyond their tormentors. The second such event is the ordeal of the handcart companies in 1856, especially the tragedy that struck the last two companies along the Sweetwater and at Devil's Gate as a result of over-optimistic leadership and under-preparation that put them on the road too late, with poor equipment, and then assumed they would make it through to the valley before snows closed the road. The dramatic rescue of the survivors by Saints from the Valley, on the other hand, demonstrates the responsiveness of the entire group once the seriousness of the events was realized.

The lives of Joe Hill and John Wesley Powell may appear at first to be far removed from Stegner's Mormon books. Yet their stories also center in Utah, and as non-Mormons they represent forces at work in the making of the American West that are quite different (and less "un-American") than the forces that molded Mormonism. Both men had dreams that, if realized, would have transformed the West. Both were rebel-reformers, agitators for change. Both were also "artists," and in the ideas and attitudes implicit in their work we find the expression of native talent, the creative thrust of folk culture. In his studies of both these men, then, Stegner continued to test his intuitions about regional character and human nature against the record of history and the facts of human and physical geography.

In "Joe Hill: The Wobblies' Troubador," an article published in the *New Republic* (Jan. 5, 1948) two years before *The Preacher and the Slave,* Stegner pointed out the reason for his interest in Hill. The illegitimate son of a Swedish nobleman who refused to recognize him (according to one legend), Hill seems to have been an itinerant seaman and world drifter until he joined up with the Wobbly movement in 1910. Why did he join, and why was he so willing to die for it four years later? According to the legend his death came as a result of a conspiracy of Mormons and "copper bosses" who feared the strength of the IWW in Utah.

Stegner's view of Joe Hill's career and of his dramatic trial and execution is quite different. Not a doctrinaire IWW, Hill was more interested in its advocacy of direct action. Hill's songs (nineteen were published in the Joe Hill Memorial Edition of the Wobbly songbook) were the artistic expression of that movement. They not only promoted the idea of One Big Union, but they also generated solidarity by bringing the men together to sing together; and they brought Hill personal recognition and an identity.

From one of these songs, "The Preacher and the Slave," Stegner takes the title of his novel. In Hill's song the distance between "the meek and humble slave" and "the preacher fat and sleek" measures the distance between worker and capitalist, exploited and exploiter (p. 227). But in the novel the preacher also refers to Hill's friend and confidant, Gus Lund, a Lutheran minister at the seamen's mission in San Pedro, California. The "slave" refers ambiguously to Joe Hill himself. Hurt during a labor dispute on the Southern Pacific in San Pedro, Hill finds sanctuary in Lund's mission. They become friends and argue over the justification of the Wobblies' program. Later, when Hill is accused in Salt Lake City of murdering a grocer and his son, Hill asks Lund to come and see him. Lund comes, feeling "like a parent brought to hear accusations against his son" (p. 255). As Bruce Mason had tried to puzzle out the paradoxes that were at the heart of his father's character, now Lund tries to puzzle out those that lie at the center of Joe Hill's.

Because the confidant Gus Lund is there, we are able to get closer to Hill than the historical record will allow us. There are his pride, his righteous indignation in insisting on a new trial and complete vindication, and his unwillingness to disclose the name of the woman who is his alibi. But we also sense, through Lund, that his zealousness and militancy are self-destructive. Hill has always liked a good fight; he cannot understand Lund's kind of charity or Lund's desire that "men . . . *whittle* their world into change and progress instead of blasting it" (p. 188).

Stegner is much more sympathetic towards John Wesley Powell, first explorer of the Colorado River, organizer and leader of the Geological Survey in Southern Utah, and dedicated exponent of federal land-reform policies during the last quarter of the Nineteenth Century. Like his friend, the sociologist Lester Ward, Powell believed man "could apply intelligence and will to his environment and bend it." The success of Powell's Colorado River expedition in 1869 was the result of "the exercise of observation, caution, intelligence, skill, planning—in a word, Science. A man or a civilization could do the same" (pp. vii-viii). No ideal could be farther from that expressed by the career of Joe Hill.

Powell's importance, writes Bernard DeVoto in his "Introduction" to the book, is that he wanted to see through the banal romantic notions of the Western experience to the underlying realities. "His career was an indomitable effort to substitute knowledge for the misconceptions and to get it acted on. He tried to repair the damage they had done to the people and the land and to prevent them from doing further damage" (p. xvi). Certainly this announces the theme of Stegner's study. Powell has Bo Mason's indomitable spirit and energy. But he is not blinded by the dream of the Big Rock Candy Mountain, nor of any of its cousins: the Mormon dream of Zion, and the Wobbly dream of solidarity forever in One Big Union.

Powell was defeated in his efforts at reform because he "underestimated the capacity of the plain dirt farmer to continue to believe in myths even while his nose was being rubbed in unpleasant fact." So he was defeated by the West itself, Western politicians, "the land and cattle and water barons, the plain homesteaders, the locally patriotic, the ambitious, the venal, the acquisitive, the myth-bound West which insisted on running into the future like a streetcar on a gravel road" (p. 338). But his failure, like that of Henry Adams, was filled with enough successes to please most men.

Wolf Willow (1962) begins as a quest for personal and cultural roots. Stegner returns to Whitemud, Saskatchewan, the scene of his youth and the setting for so many of his stories, to test his memory against the knowing mind. "I may not know who I am," he says, "but I know where I came from" (p. 23). The return is to a certain place: the prairies and a prairie town. But he is made aware—upon actually returning—of the fallibility and capriciousness of memory as well as its power to make things unforgettable. The pungent and pervasive odor of Wolf Willow along the banks of the river, an odor that he can faintly recall but not for a time identify, makes him realize that "the sensuous little savage" in him is still there (p. 19).

But such memories are not a substitute for history; as history, "[memories] have the lurid explosiveness of a prairie fire, quickly dangerous, swiftly over." Memories are deceptive and are not long enough—do not reach far enough. He feels the need to correct what the child sees with what the adult knows, or has imagined, or heard about—the need "to make perception serve inference"—and place his vivid but personal memories in some broader, justifying and confirming context (pp. 4-9).

In the second section of *Wolf Willow*, "Preparation For a Civilization," Stegner moves from personal reminiscence to a history of the region. Section three, "The Whitemud Range," examines the relationship of character to environment, economic and geographic. "It was a nearly womanless culture, nomadic, harsh, dangerous, essentially romantic" (p. 135). Two stories, "Genesis" and "Carrion Spring," develop the themes of the making of a man and the disillusionment of a woman respectively. But Stegner's final judgment of the culture is neither nostalgic nor romantic. The fourth and fifth sections of the book—ironically prefaced by quotations from Josiah Royce's *The Hope of the Great Community* and Sinclair Lewis' *Main Street*—point out the many cultural limitations of the small town in the sparsely populated West. And the "Making of Paths" is a nostalgic recalling of a boy's life on a prairie homestead that is at once an idyl and a failure. Nostalgia is not enough. Whitemud was a good place to be a boy, a bad place to be a man.

V

The first of Wallace Stegner's two volumes of collected short stories, *The Women on the Wall* (1950), contains several stories that come from his boyhood experiences in Saskatchewan, many of which were incorporated into *The Big Rock Candy Mountain*. Two that were not, "The Chink" (a study of a boy's intimate attachment to a "foreigner") and "In the Twilight," are still stories featuring "Bruce" or a boy who could be Bruce. They center around some incident that opens the boy's eyes to his world; they are filled with a sensitive child's awe, pain, and pleasure. There is the terrible disappointment of a car's not starting and thereby preventing the family's long anticipated trip to the fourth of July celebration in "Goin' to Town." There is the compensatory picnic in "Two Rivers" where his mother ponders the things that stick in a child's memory. Trapping gophers in "Bugle Song" and killing a sow in "In the Twilight," part of the homesteader's routine, become events of magnitude —and the boy, overcome with fascinated horror, learns to maintain the distance from any torturous death that is necessary to bear it. In "The Colt" the boy's forgetfulness contributes to the crippling and finally the death of his colt. A very masculine father and a sacrificed, patient mother figure in nearly all the stories; bits of both are found in the boy.

The other stories vary in theme. Two depict women with husbands home on furlough or away at war. "The Berry Patch" is almost pastoral—a farm wife seeks to please her husband and assure him that she can carry on without him. In "The Women on the Wall" a male observer watches several war wives and learns that these modern Penelopes are not so virtuous or gracious as the wife who waited twenty years for Odysseus. He seems almost callous in cataloging their major and minor failings as they all wait for mail "on the wall."

In "A View from the Balcony" married graduate students living together in a final kind of wartime camaraderie give a party in which the perils of civilian life, including professional jealousy and potential failure, are uncovered, and a young English war bride senses real lions and tigers in the pastoral civilian fields. Another story reveals with precise economy the human tragedy of an unhappy marriage as a successful young scientist visits an old college friend, who feigns alcoholic incomprehension in order to avoid any straight talk about his empty life and his faithless wife—he is "Beyond a Glass Mountain."

In the most touching story in *The City of the Living* (1956), "The Blue-Winged Teal," a young man learns that his despised father has depths of feeling about his dead mother that he had not suspected. Other conflicts between parents and children are developed in "The Volunteer," where a boy finds recognition at school and rejection from his father, and "Impasse," in which a father senses his unlovely daughter's frustrations but is helpless to communicate his understanding or to solve her strident demands.

Two stories look back in time. A young man returns to Salt Lake City to tend to a dead relative's affairs and finds that the funeral home is located in an old house, a former haunt of his in college when a lovely young girl lived there. The dead past comes alive when he stands in the old rooms and ponders the directions his life might have taken had he acted differently toward the "Maiden in a Tower." "The Traveler" reveals a kind of mystic communion between a traveling salesman whose car is stalled on a lonely snowy night and a boy in a farm house caring for an old ill grandfather. In the boy, he sees himself as a boy, anxious for wider prospects but held away from them.

Weak or antagonistic communications between old and young are the themes again of "The City of the Living," in which a father traveling in Egypt fears for the life of his fever-wracked son and sorts out his lonely affairs in the foreign night. In the longest story, published as a novella, "The Field Guide to Western Birds," a retired literary agent is the main character. Joe Allston will appear again, his acerbic humor intensified, in *All the Little Live Things*. Allston describes the California foothills where he has retired—its bird, animal, and human life. In this story he regretfully unmasks a talented charlatan, the star of a neighbor's benefit party, "a cuckoo chick in a robin's nest."

Except for this wry humor, both volumes of short stories are marked by a general absence of laughter. In "The Volunteer" the boy says that laughter is not a solution for his family in a crisis. The stories indicate with compassion the barriers that people erect or simply find between one another, barriers that frequently cannot be articulated or expunged or laughed away.

The most powerful characteristic of all is that no matter where the story is set, Stegner draws the scene and places us in it so securely that the idea of the story can never come to us without the setting—a clear cold King Wenceslaus night in the snow, an oppressive room in a blue-black Egyptian night, the rainless prairie of Saskatchewan, a table on the Riviera waterfront, a "family" duckfeed in a bleak, windowless, smelly poolroom. It is the scene that sets the mood and prepares the way for human action. In this sense all his stories are regional and all the regions recognizable.

VI

Stegner has said that he has never written about California in the way that land becomes a character ("Conversations with Wallace Stegner," *South Dakota Review,* Spring 1971), "because I don't feel this country the way I would feel the short grass plains or the Rocky Mountains" (p. 49). California is not the West in that sense; it is frontier and dream—the shining vision that brought people like the Joads from Oklahoma in endless procession like agrarian gold miners.

California seems on the edge of things. "Across the mountain," says Joe Allston in *All the Little Live Things* (1967), "the pale air swept in from remote places—Hawaii, Midway, illimitable Japans. I have never anywhere else had so strong a feeling of the vast continuity of the air in which we live" (p. 17). The scope of thought is broadened. A hawk in a eucalyptus tree stares at Allston in his garden, "wondering what I was doing. . . . It was a fair question and I could have answered it. I was pondering the vanity of human wishes and the desperation of human hope, the tooth of time, the vulnerability of good and the unseen omnipresence of evil and the frailty and passion of life. That is all I was pondering" (p. 7).

Stegner in these novels examines Americans brought up short against the sea, turned in on themselves, living "in the shape of tomorrow" without much comprehension of the past. The narrator of the last novel, *Angle of Repose* (1971), is a retired historian whose son, Rodman, a sociologist, never looks back farther than ten years. "My grandparents' lives seem to me organic," says the historian, "and ours what? hydroponic?" (p. 18). (The term refers to the soilless growth of plants.)

The heroine of *A Shooting Star* (1961), set mainly in the Bay area of California, suffers from precisely this kind of modern rootlessness. Childless, married to a rich society doctor, Burke Castro, her sense of uselessness drives her to an illicit affair which deeply troubles her. She leaves her husband and goes back to her mother's home.

Finding purpose in life and translating it into action absorbs Sabrina and most of the other characters in the novel. Sabrina, on a spree, tells her brother how "lucky" pioneer women were. "I wish Burke had been driving a covered wagon when I met him" (p. 161). She pictures herself driving away Indians with a Sharps rifle and making soap over a greasewood fire. She scorns her mother's "usefulness": a transplanted wealthy Bostonian, her mother labors to preserve her Eastern family's history—a family excruciatingly materialistic, unimaginative, and unproductive.

The rich have a harder time feeling useful than struggling Leonard MacDonald, who has married one of Sabrina's friends. He teaches high school, wears blue jeans even when hired to restore the books and papers in Sabrina's mother's archives, and is full of purpose. He tells Sabrina that wealth is not the cause of her family's historic lack of accomplishment—but that it is caused by "paralysis of the will," a disease his blue-collar father had, too.

Leonard in his spare time keeps his old car and his young family going and joins a committee to get a park set aside in a new development. We note with uneasiness the absence of wildness in Leonard's tract house life in Greenwood Acres, celled with little family units, looped back on itself, as "peripheral . . . and as subject to infection as a veriform appendix. Nevertheless the true social shape of the future" (p. 202).

Leonard comes to the defense of this overcrowded latter-day Utopia when a scornful Sabrina attacks it. Aware that none of his family ever had the dimmest notion of history, literature, or art, he can appreciate a middle class with upward aspirations. And he has a sense that his job, teaching, matters, even at a paltry salary. MacDonald is almost incredible in his self-satisfaction.

The original conflict in the novel, Sabrina's anguished sense of guilt, gives way to her resolutions at the end—to keep and raise the illegitimate child on the way, and to aid her failing, lonely mother to ease the change from the great estate to the subdivision process that greedy brother Oliver has engineered, and to provide a part of that estate for Leonard's city park. These are hardly great cries for personal liberation. They are rather the old themes of familial and community concern. Stegner's main characters in this novel are finally willing to settle for "halfway decent lives," willed to be so. So are the characters in the next two novels.

What frustrates successful, retired literary agent Joe Allston in *All the Little Live Things* is that living a halfway decent life was enough to make him happy, but it was not enough for his son, whose death, possibly suicide, Allston has come to the California hills to grieve. Curtis, who ended up in California, a surf bum at thirty-seven, actively rejected all Joe's values. Joe, who came up the hard way from Iowa to Madison Avenue, cannot see what he could have done differently, but nevertheless he has sleepless, solitary nights haunted by the ghosts of his hardworking immigrant mother, who sacrificed everything for him, and of his son who never worked at all.

Joe is middle America, but he laughs at himself in the midst of his pain and is far more sensitive than most behind his ironic wisecracking shell. He is more than willing to share his sense of parental failure with the American society that encouraged his son "to hunt out the shoddy, the physical, the self-indulgent . . . and call these things freedom" (p. 178). He is, he insists, a Roman Stoic who prefers austere republics to decadent empires.

He also believes in cultivating his garden; and all the gophers Wallace Stegner ever poisoned on the Saskatchewan homestead are resurrected in those two that gnaw down Joe's blossoming cherry tree. Attacking them, he inadvertently kills a king snake which has just swallowed one of the gophers (another image Stegner has planted in two different novels). This gopher-killing Manichean finds the good snake ambiguous. "Mischance is a collaboration. . . . evil is everywhere. Yet I am steadily tempted to poke around in the garden, looking for the snake. Sooner or later I shall find myself going (coming?) down my hole after myself. . . . None of us is truly harmless" (p. 92).

Joe finds this especially true of an intruding hippy type, who camps on Joe's land after getting his grudging permission. Caliban, Joe calls him, a Dionysian figure. Peck takes advantage of Joe's unwilling generosity, scattering garbage, hooking into Joe's water and electricity, inviting other transients to share his good fortune, generally spreading like the poison oak he has agreed to grub out but does not. When Marian sweetly calls him a homesteader, Joe applies the pejorative: "Squatter. Nester" (p. 160). Joe most dislikes Peck's assumption that his way of life is semi-saintly.

Then Joe finds someone he regards as truly harmless in a new neighbor, Marian Catlin, with her husband and small daughter. Pregnant, glowing with life, she enchants Joe as the daughter he never had, Prospero's Miranda. Her ecstatic belief in goodness and the progress of undisturbed nature strikes Joe as "unnatural," even while she coaxes him out of his ironic shell. When the Allstons learn that she is dying of cancer, Joe curses again the unknowable forces that conspire against goodness and fruition.

"Crabby, hippy, and happy," one reviewer (*New York Times,* August 6, 1967, p. 30) irreverently described the three principal characters. There is an element of distortion involved in seeing all through Joe's conservative eyes. Marian is too good; and we never really know Jim Peck, the seedy rebel against the Establishment, Order, and Authority, except from the distance that both he and Allston instinctively agree to keep—practicing yoga in his tree house, remaining aloof from a neighborhood work party. It is Jim Peck's unneighborliness that finally cannot be forgiven. In searching for new communal values he has neglected the old ones. While Marian listens eagerly and tolerantly to Peck expound his new educational theories, he has not learned the elemental facts about her. His communication is one way.

In a superbly climatic final scene that brings every young neighbor and the exiled Jim Peck to a startling confrontation, old Joe Allston makes his final condemnation of the young of the society he disapproves: " 'Unthought, Irresponsibility, Rebellion, and Foolishness!' held a conference or a quarrel and blocked the road" (p. 331). Marian's last glimpse of the unspoiled nature she loves, as Joe drives her to the hospital to die, is a scene of chaotic destruction. Joe, a furious, sad, believable Everyman demands that we all, young and old, acknowledge our potential harmfulness in the threatened, tenuous human community.

The third novel in this group, *Angle of Repose,* is so ambitious in its scope and setting that it compares more than well with *The Big Rock Candy Mountain.* While the latter is Western, *Angle of*

Repose embraces the continent. Its characters, four generations of them, treated realistically, gradually grow larger than life to illustrate ideas about the country we live in and the conflicting ways we live in it.

In *Angle of Repose* the main metaphor is scientific—the term "angle of repose" is the geological term for the diminished incline that halts a landslide, and is used because the historian-narrator's grandfather is a mining engineer. Lyman Ward, the narrator, is interested in Time and the relation of Past to Present; he is willing to learn from his grandparents, whose marriage symbolizes for him the tension of uneasy opposites—"unlike particles" —which come to rest at last in the California cottage where he first knows them. His interest is personal because his own marriage is at loose ends, and it is historical because he clearly sees in his grandparents the conflicts of the genteel East and the pioneering West personified.

The narrator-participant is a grotesque figure. Confined to a wheelchair with a crippling bone disease, he is holed up in the cottage his grandparents built. There he is cared for by a loyal housekeeper who had cared for his father and whose avant-garde daughter serves as temporary secretary. In the same methodical way he goes through his limited physical regime he goes through their collected letters and papers, distilling his grandparents' lives and his own thoughts on tape.

His grandmother was Susan Burling Ward, talented author-illustrator of Quaker background, who leaves her genteel artistic circle in New York in 1870 to marry and go West with Oliver Ward, a mining engineer, an unlikely relative of the New England Wards and Beechers. She always expects to go back East, refusing to realize that a mining engineer has no place to go but West. She pours her exile's heart into her letters to her bosom friend, Augusta (the intensity of their attachment startles Lyman). Augusta's husband, an editor of *Scribner's,* epitomizes Susan's real ideal; he is fragile, refined, intellectual—Eastern.

Susan struggles to draw illustrations for *The Scarlet Letter* in the West, but finally realizes that her fortune will lie in drawing and writing stories about the West itself—fortunately, because her success at it will support the couple and three children through Oliver's successive disappointments in California, Colorado, Mexico, and Idaho. His manly idealism and complete honesty are disadvantages in the rough West, and his visionary schemes are usually premature. They lack the capital or mechanical advances to implement the projects. He invents concrete, but someone else will patent it, and his design for an irrigation project must wait for later government capital to develop. Oliver always loses because he is ahead of his time; he reminds us of John Wesley Powell, rather than Bo Mason.

The great canal he seeks to build near Boise, Idaho—the last and most crushing of their defeats, and the personal events connected with it—cost them all future peace of mind and leave them a marriage based on a "false arch," the cornerstone of complete faith crumbled, the cement of forgiveness unperfected. Both of his grandparents failed personally—Susan in her over-emphasis on gentility that led her to underestimate the different talents of her husband and to alienate her son while "saving him" from the West—and Oliver, in his uncompromising inarticulateness.

The careful writing that produces setting after setting of keen realism—the Quaker farm in Milton, New York, the cheerless frontier town of the Dakotas, a comfortable cottage in New Almaden, a boarding house in Santa Cruz, a rude cabin in Leadville, Colorado (where Susan "holds court" for writers Helen Hunt Jackson, Clarence King, and others), a Mexican compound, a stone shack in the Idaho canyons—is Stegner at his observant, creative best. "Experience new-minted," not historical pageant, as one reviewer put it (William Abrahams, "The Real Thing," *Atlantic,* April 1971, p. 96). Stegner has had help in the Stanford Library collection of letters, articles, and novels of Mary Hallock Foote, the model for the character of Susan Ward.

Yet in this "realistic" novel lies a surreal and satirical quality freely adopted in *All the Little Live Things,* and evident in the modern characters here: a paralytic historian who can look in only one direction, a loud harassing sociologist son who is not sure what history is for, a brassy braless secretary chortling at Lyman Ward's Victorian grandmother's modesty or finding great originality in her boy friend's idea for a commune, never having heard of Oneida or Brook Farm. The Present seems less real than the Past. The narrator's situation is at once more comic and more grievous than his grandparents'. His wife has run away with the surgeon who took off his leg, and he cannot get both feet back on the ground.

VII

It is impossible to place Stegner in any of the several literary traditions that have dominated twentieth-century prose writing. His insistence that the basis for fiction lies in personal experience and his use of the techniques of impressionistic realism—as well as his belief that the subject of fiction is the conduct of individuals —suggest that his own work, both in its conception and in its craftsmanship, has roots that go back to Henry James, Joseph Conrad, F. Scott Fitzgerald, and Ernest Hemingway.

In an essay published in the March 1950 *Yale Review* ("Variations on a Theme by Conrad") Stegner offered the following manifesto:

> I am convinced that literature has as its primary aim
> the celebration of the human spirit as that spirit works
> itself out in conduct, and I am convinced that because of
> its peculiar capacity to explore the problems of conduct
> at length the novel is potentially the noblest of our liter-
> ary forms.   (p. 522)

Stegner is concerned in this essay that the totalitarian mind looks at humanity in the mass, rather than as individuals, as do many contemporary novelists. Stegner is a moralist, not a behaviorist. He does not accept the tenets of the naturalistic tradition.

Stegner has identified himself intellectually with the vernacular tradition of native frontier humor and Western journalism of the late Nineteenth Century, the tradition that realized a genius such as Mark Twain. But he admits that this tradition died under the pressure of "gloomy philosophy" imported from abroad, the destruction of a homogeneous American society by industrialism and immigration, and the discovery that "human nature was a little too perverse" to fulfill the expectations of the American democratic dream upon which it thrived.

Stegner has never had much sympathy for any of the traditions that have replaced this first, native one. He finds especially repugnant the despair that characterizes the so-called modern tradition. "There is no pessimist like a disappointed optimist, no despair like that of a chronically hopeful man" ("The American Literary Tradition," *The Writer in America,* pp. 31-33). One way out of the chronic despair is to get rid of the chronic optimism. Another way out is to realize the intellectual dead-end of such pessimism. "We have so mourned the ugly duckling of a society we have raised, so bewailed its lack of resemblance to Aunt Victoria or Uncle Utopia, that we have missed the emerging swan" ("Is the Novel Done For?" *Harper's,* Dec. 1942, p. 81). Stegner has always been committed intellectually to the "emerging swan," and in this sense at least he shows both his liberalism and his humanism.

Yet his strongest writing concerns people who live in a world fed more by failure than hope, people caught between the known shapes of the past and the still unknown shape of the future. "Before I can say I *am,* I was," he has Lyman Ward say on the opening page of *Angle of Repose.* "Heraclitus and I, prophets of flux, know that the flux is composed of parts that imitate and repeat each other. Am or was, I am cumulative, too. I am everything I ever was." Lyman Ward, like Stegner, believes in "life chronological," not "life existential" (pp. 1, 8).

If the past is largely responsible for the shape of the present, the writer must go in search of a usable past—a past that will help him find some ordering principle in current change. The problems related to the writer's search for a usable past Stegner analyzes in the essays collected in the last part of *The Sound of Mountain Water* (1969). Although he has admired the work of such regional writers as A. B. Guthrie and Walter Van Tilburg Clark, Stegner finds that only Wright Morris has examined the changing contemporary regional experience with the passion of a James Baldwin or a William Faulkner. Western writers continue to "live in exile and write of anguishes not our own, or content ourselves with the bland troubles, the remembered violences, the already enduring hardships of a regional success story without the aftermath" (p. 49).

That word *aftermath* tells us something about the essential flavor of Stegner's fictional world at its best. The parallel that Stegner implies exists between his own work and that of Baldwin is significant. While one writes of the Black experience and the other the Western experience, both believe that the present is shaped by the past. Both believe that the freedom to explore future possibilities requires first that their people recognize and accept as real those forces that have created their present condition. And both writers have worked out the relationship of past and present in the relations of fathers and sons.

Another relationship which has concerned Stegner because he believes it helps explain the human condition in both its actual and potential forms is the relationship of character to landscape. We have mentioned his warning to young writers not to get carried away with the Western scenery. Since Stegner has himself written movingly of the landscape, this advice is perhaps puzzling.

A place is nothing in itself. It has no meaning, it can hardly be said to exist, except in terms of human perception, use, and response. The wealth and resources and usefulness of any region are only inert potential until man's hands and brain have gone to work; and natural beauty is nothing until it comes to the eye of the beholder. The natural world, actually, is the test by which each man proves himself: I see, I feel, I love, I use, I alter, I appropriate, therefore I am. Or the natural world is a screen onto which we project our own images; without our images there, it is as blank as the cold screen of an empty movie house. ("The Marks of Human Passage," *This is Dinosaur,* p. 15)

As with the past, the writer's shaping of the landscape is a way of shaping the larger world of which he is a part. Stegner has been interested in the relationship of the artist to the landscape since, in the mid-1930's, he wrote his Iowa thesis on Clarence Edward Dutton, Powell's co-worker in geology.

The essays on the wilderness collected in the first part of *The Sound of Mountain Water* indicate the range of Stegner's responses to nature. It can be a personal and impressionistic experience in "The Sound of Mountain Water," graphically evocative in "The Rediscovery of America: 1946" and "Packhorse Paradise," reflective in "Glen Canyon Submersus," and philosophical and prophetic in the "Wilderness Letter," where he argues that the wilderness is the "geography of hope." "We need wilderness preserved—as much as is still left, and as many kinds— because it was the challenge against which our character as a people was formed" (p. 147). Yet the wilderness with which he is most familiar, the semi-arid, Rocky Mountain West, is also an "oasis civilization." "*Limitation, deprivation,* are words we must

keep in mind when speaking of the reputedly limitless West."
If the mountains represent the "quintessential West," the desert
is "the truest West, its dead and arid heart" (pp. 10-14) .

Selected Bibliography

BOOKS BY STEGNER

All the Little Live Things. New York: Viking Press, 1967.

Angle of Repose. New York: Doubleday, 1971.

Beyond the Hundredth Meridian: John Wesley Powell and the Second Opening of the West. Boston: Houghton Mifflin, 1954.

The Big Rock Candy Mountain. New York: Duell, Sloan and Pearce, 1943.

The City of the Living and Other Stories. Boston: Houghton Mifflin, 1956.

Fire and Ice. New York: Duell, Sloan and Pearce, 1941.

The Gathering of Zion. New York: McGraw-Hill Book Co., 1964.

Mormon Country. New York: Bonanza Books, 1942.

On a Darkling Plain. New York: Harcourt, 1940.

One Nation, with the editors of *Look Magazine*. Boston: Houghton Mifflin, 1945.

The Potter's House. Muscatine, Iowa: The Prairie Press, 1938.

The Preacher and the Slave. Boston: Houghton Mifflin, 1950.

Remembering Laughter. Boston: Little Brown and Co., 1937.

Second Growth. Boston: Houghton Mifflin, 1947.

A Shooting Star. New York: Viking Press, 1961.

The Sound of Mountain Water. Garden City, New York: Doubleday, Inc., 1969.

Wolf Willow: A History, a Story, and a Memory of the Last Plains Frontier. New York: Viking Press, 1962.

The Women on the Wall. Boston: Houghton Mifflin, 1950.

The Writer in America. Tokyo: Hokuseido Press, 1952; rpt. Folcroft, Pa.: Folcroft Press, 1951.

CURRENT AMERICAN REPRINTS IN PAPERBACK

All the Little Live Things. New York: Signet (New American Library), 1968.

Beyond the Hundredth Meridian: John Wesley Powell and the Second Opening of the West. Boston: Sentry Edition (Houghton Mifflin), 1962.

The Big Rock Candy Mountain. New York: American Century (Hill and Wang) , 1957.

Joe Hill. New York: Ballantine, 1972. Rpt. of *The Preacher and the Slave.* Boston: Houghton Mifflin, 1950.

Wolf Willow: A History, a Story, and a Memory of the Last Plains Frontier. New York: Compass Books (Viking Press) , 1962.

SHORT STORIES BY STEGNER

"Admirable Crichton." *New Yorker,* 22 (June 15, 1946) , 52.

"All the Little Live Things." *Mademoiselle,* 49 (May 1959) , 90-91.

"Angle of Repose." *McCalls,* 98 (April 1971) , 103-10.

"Balance His, Swing Yours." *Rocky Mountain Review,* 10 (Autumn 1945) , 32-38.

"Berry Patch." *Atlantic,* 172 (September 1943) , 51-53.

"Beyond the Glass Mountain." *Harper's,* 194 (May 1947) , 446-52.

"Bloodstain." *American Prefaces,* 2 (Summer 1937) , 150-53.

"Blue-Winged Teal." *Harper's,* 200 (April 1950) , 41-49.

"Bugle Song." *Virginia Quarterly Review,* 14 (July 1938) , 407-15.

"Butcher Bird." *Harper's,* 182 (January 1941) , 156-63.

"Carrion Spring." *Esquire,* 58 (October 1962) , 130.

"The Chink." *Atlantic,* 166 (September 1940) , 349-56.

"Chip Off the Old Block." *Virginia Quarterly Review,* 18 (October 1942) , 573-90.

"City of the Living." *Mademoiselle,* 38 (January 1954) , 78-79.

"The Colt." *Southwest Review,* 28 (Autumn 1942—Summer, 1943) , 267-79.

"Genesis." *Contact,* 2 (1959) , 85-86.

"Goin' to Town." *Atlantic,* 165 (June 1940) , 770-76.

"Hostage." *Virginia Quarterly Review,* 19 (July 1943) , 403-11.

"House on Cherry Creek." *Colliers,* 116 (August 11, 1945) , 16-17.

"Maiden in a Tower." *Harper's,* 208 (January 1954) , 78-84.

"Pop Goes the Alley Cat." *Harper's,* 204 (February 1952) , 42-52.

"The Potter's House." *American Prefaces,* 3 (Summer 1938) , 147-51.

"Saw Gang." *Atlantic,* 176 (October 1945) , 82-84.

"The Traveler." *Harper's,* 202 (February 1951) , 79-84.

"Turtle at Home." *Atlantic,* 171 (April 1943) , 123, 127.

"Two Rivers." *Atlantic,* 169 (June 1942) , 745-52.

"The Volcano." *Harper's,* 189 (September 1944) , 315-18.

"Volunteer." *Mademoiselle,* 43 (October 1956) , 124-25, 146-56.

"Wolfer." *Harper's,* 209 (October 1959) , 53-61.

"The Women on the Wall." *Harper's,* 192 (April 1946) , 366-79.

44

ESSAYS, ARTICLES, AND REVIEWS BY STEGNER

"America's Mightiest Playground." *Holiday,* 20 (July 1956), 34-43.

"The American People Against the American Continent." *Vermont History,* 35 (1967), 177-85.

"Backroads River." *Atlantic,* 181 (January 1948), 59-64.

"Battle for the Wilderness." *New Republic,* 130 (February 15, 1954), 13-15.

"The Book and the Great Community." *Library Journal,* 93 (October 1, 1968), 3513-16.

"Born a Square: The Westerners' Dilemma." *Atlantic,* 213 (January 1964), 46-50.

"C. E. Dutton, Explorer, Geologist, Nature Writer." *Scientific Monthly,* 45 (July 1937), 82-85.

"California: The Experimental Society." *Saturday Review,* 50, (September 23, 1967), 28,

"Celebrated Jumping Freud." *Reporter,* 22 (March 17, 1960), 45-46.

"Child of the Far Frontier." *Horizon,* 5 (September 1962), 94-95.

"Conservation Equals Survival." *American Heritage,* 21 (December 1969), 12-15.

"Fiction: A Lense on Life." *Saturday Review,* 33 (April 22, 1950), 9-10, 32-33.

"Foreword" to *The Big Sky* by A. B. Guthrie, Jr. Boston: Sentry (Houghton Mifflin), 1965.

"Get Out of That Story!" *Writer,* 56 (December 1943), 360-62.

"Good-bye to All t--t!" *Atlantic,* 215 (March 1965), 119.

"History Comes to the Plains." *American Heritage,* 8 (June 1957), 14-15, 15-19, 108-11.

"History, Myth, and the Western Writer." *American West,* 4 (1967), 61-62, 76-79. Rpt. as "Introduction" to *Great Western Short Stories.* Ed. J. Golden Taylor. Palo Alto: American West Publishing Co., 1967.

"Introduction." *The Outcasts of Poker Flat and Other Tales* by Bret Harte. New York: Signet (New American Library), 1961. Rpt. as "The West Synthetic: Bret Harte" in *The Sound of Mountain Water.*

"Introduction." *Selected American Prose, 1841-1900: The Realistic Movement.* Ed. Wallace Stegner. New York: Holt, Rinehart and Winston, 1958. Pp. v-xxvi.

"Is the Novel Done For?" *Harper's,* 186 (December 1942), 76-83.

"Joe Hill: The Wobblies' Troubadour." *New Republic,* 118 (January 5, 1948), 20-25.

"Love Affair With the Heber Valley, U.S.A." *Vogue,* 131 (February 1, 1958), 132-33.

"Making of Paths." *New Yorker,* 34 (September 6, 1958), 37-38.

"The Marks of Human Passage." *This is Dinosaur.* Ed. Wallace Stegner. New York: Alfred A. Knopf, 1955. Pp. 3-17.

"Megalopolis and the Country All Around." *Living Wilderness,* 82 (Winter 1962) , 23-24.

"Mounties at Fort Walsh." *Atlantic,* 202 (July 1958) , 50-54.

"Myths of the Western Dam." *Saturday Review,* 48 (October 23, 1965) , 29-31.

"On Censorship." *Arts in Society,* 4 (Summer 1967) , 281-99.

"On the Writing of History." *American West,* 2 (1965) , 6-13. Rpt. in *The Sound of Mountain Water.*

"One-fourth of a Nation; Public Lands and Itching Fingers." *Reporter,* 8 (May 12, 1953) , 25-29.

"One Last Wilderness." *Scribner's,* 105 (January 1939) , 16.

"One Way to Spell Man." *Saturday Review,* 41 (May 24, 1958) , 8-11, 43-44.

"Ordeal at Devil's Gate." *Esquire,* 41 (June 1964) , 100-101.

"Ordeal by Handcart." *Collier's,* 138 (July 6, 1956) , 78-85.

"Packhorse Paradise." *Atlantic,* 180 (September 1947) , 21-26.

"The Personality [of Bernard DeVoto]" in *Four Portraits and One Subject.* Ed. Catherine Drinker Bowen. Boston: Houghton Mifflin, 1963. Rpt. as "The West Emphatic: Bernard DeVoto" in *The Sound of Mountain Water.*

"A Pioneer Record." *Southwest Review,* 24 (July 1939) , 369-87. Rpt. as "Notes on a Life Spent Picking at a Sandstone Cliff" in *Mormon Country.*

"Powell and the Names on the Plateau." *Western Humanities Review,* 7 (Spring 1953) , 105-10. Rpt. as "Names" in *Beyond the Hundredth Meridian.*

"Quiet Earth, Big Sky." *American Heritage,* 6 (October 1955) , 22-27.

"Renaissance in Many Tongues." *Saturday Review,* 34 (August 4, 1951) , 27-28, 52-53.

"Shaping of Experience." *Writer,* 55 (April 1942) , 99-102.

"To a Young Writer." *Atlantic,* 204 (November 1959) , 88-91.

"Town Dump." *Atlantic,* 204 (October 1959) , 78-80. Rpt. as "The Dump Ground" in *Wolf Willow.*

"Truth and Faking in Fiction." *Writer,* 53 (February 1940) , 40-43.

"Variations on a Theme by Conrad." *Yale Review,* 39 (March 1950) , 512-23.

"Western Record and Romance." *Literary History of the United States.* Ed. Robert E. Spiller et al. 3rd ed., rev. New York: Macmillan, 1963. Pp. 862-77.

"Who Persecutes Boston?" *Atlantic,* 174 (July 1944) , 45-52.

"The Wilderness Idea." *Wilderness: America's Living Heritage.* Ed. David Brower. San Francisco: Sierra Club, 1961. Pp. 97-102. Rpt. as "The Meaning of Wilderness in American Civilization" in *The American Environment Readings in the History of Conservation.* Ed. Roderick Nash. Reading, Mass.: Addison-Wesley, 1968. Pp. 192-97. Rpt. as "Coda: Wilderness Letter" in *The Sound of Mountain Water.* Rpt. as "Wilderness

Letter" in *The Literature of the American West*. Ed. J. Golden Taylor. Boston: Houghton Mifflin, 1971. Pp. 446-50.

"Willa Cather: *My Ántonia*." *The American Novel: From James Fenimore Cooper to William Faulkner*. Ed. Wallace Stegner. Rpt. as "The West Authentic: Willa Cather" in *The Sound of Mountain Water*.

INTERVIEWS, CRITICAL STUDIES, AND REVIEWS

Abbey, Edward. "What's the Place of the Western Writer?" Review of *The Sound of Mountain Water*. *N. Y. Times Book Review*, June 8, 1969, p. 10.

Abrahams, William. "The Real Thing." Review of *Angle of Repose*. *Atlantic*, 228 (April 1971), 96-97.

Adams, Frank S. "American Minorities." Review of *One Nation*. *N. Y. Times Book Review*, October 7, 1945, p. 5.

Baker, Carlos. "Too Much of Everything." Review of *A Shooting Star*. *N. York Times Book Review*, May 21, 1961, p. 5.

Beach, Joseph Warren. "Life-Size Stegner." Review of *The Big Rock Candy Mountain*. *N. Y. Times Book Review*, September 26, 1943, p. 4.

Buitenhuis, Peter. "Sunset Years in the West." Review of *All the Little Live Things*. *N. Y. Times Book Review*, August 6, 1967, pp. 5, 30.

Cadle, Dean. "Man and Ozymandias." Review of *Beyond the Hundredth Meridian*. *Western Review*, 20 (Autumn 1955), 75-77.

Clayton, James L. "From Provincials: Mormonism as Seen by Wallace Stegner." *Dialogues: American Journal of Mormon Thought*, 1 (1966), 105-14.

Corle, Edwin. "A Great Man When Our West Was Young." Review of *Beyond the Hundredth Meridian*. *N. Y. Herald Tribune Book Reviews*, September 19, 1954, p. 4.

Culligan, Glendy. Review of *Angle of Repose*. *Saturday Review*, 54 (March 20, 1971), 29, 34.

Davis, R. G. "Voices Speaking from the Lonely Crowd." Review of *City of the Living*. *N. Y. Times Book Review*, October 28, 1956, p. 6.

Eisinger, C. E. "Twenty Years of Wallace Stegner." *College English*, 20 (December 1958), 110-16.

———. "Wallace Stegner: The Uncommitted." *Fiction of the Forties*. Chicago: University of Chicago Press, 1963. Pp. 324-28.

Gray, James. "Stegner's Short Stories." Review of *City of the Living*. *N. Y. Herald Tribune Book Reviews*, November 4, 1956, p. 4.

Harlow, Robert. "Whitemud Revisited." Review of *Wolf Willow*. *Canadian Literature*, (1963), 63-66.

Hicks, Granville. "Fiction That Grows from the Ground." Includes a review of *All the Little Live Things*. *Saturday Review,* 50 (August 5, 1967), 23-24.

Hudson, Lois Phillips. "*The Big Rock Candy Mountain:* No Roots and No Frontier." *S. Dakota Review,* 9 (Spring 1971), 3-13.

Jones, Howard Mumford. Review of *The Big Rock Candy Mountain. Saturday Review,* 26 (October 2, 1943), 10.

Lehman, Milton G. "New Generation." Review of *On a Darkling Plain. New Republic,* 102 (February 26, 1940), 284.

Lyne, Peter. "Ethan Frome in Iowa." Review of *Remembering Laughter. Christian Science Monitor,* October 13, 1937, p. 14.

Lyon, T. Edgar. Review of *The Gathering of Zion. Western Humanities Review,* 19 (Summer 1965), 279-80.

Milton, John, ed. and comp. "Conversation with Wallace Stegner." *S. Dakota Review,* 9 (Spring 1971), 45-57.

Peden, William. "Bruce, a Sensitive Boy, and Life." Review of *The Women on the Wall. Saturday Review,* 33 (January 21, 1950), 17.

Sandoz, Mari. "Prophet of the Far West." Review of *Beyond the Hundredth Meridian. Saturday Review,* 37 (September 11, 1954), 36.

Sorensen, Virginia. "Deserts and Mountains and Green Valleys." Review of *Mormon Country. N. Y. Herald Tribune Book Reviews,* October 11, 1942, p. 3.

Stafford, Jean. "How the West is Being Lost." Review of *The Sound of Mountain Water. Book World,* June 1, 1969, p. 4.

Stewart, George R. "Land of the Mormons." Review of *Mormon Country. N. Y. Times Book Review,* October 25, 1942, p. 20.

Whipple, Maurine. "Mormon Folklore." Review of *Mormon Country. Saturday Review,* 26 (January 2, 1943), 21.